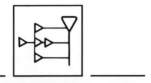

SCIENCE IN
ANCIENT MESOPOTAMIA

CAROL MOSS

SCIENCE IN ANCIENT MESOPOTAMIA

A First Book
Franklin Watts   1988
New York   London   Toronto   Sydney

Library of Congress Cataloging-in-Publication Data

Moss, Carol (Carol Marie)

Science in ancient Mesopotamia/Carol Moss.
p.   cm.—(A First book)
Bibliography: p.
Includes index.
Summary: Describes the enormous accomplishments of the Sumerians
and Babylonians of ancient Mesopotamia in every scientific area, a
heritage which affects our own everyday lives.
ISBN 0-531-10594-6
1. Science—Iraq—History—Juvenile literature. 2. Science,
Ancient—Juvenile literature. 3. Iraq—Civilization—To 634—
Juvenile literature. 4. Sumerians—History—Juvenile literature.
[1. Science—Iraq—History. 2. Science, Ancient. 3. Iraq—
Civilization—To 634. 4. Sumerians—History.] I. Title.
Q127.I7M67   1988   88-2661
509.35—dc19   CIP   AC

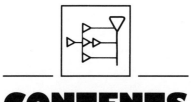

CONTENTS

SCIENCE IN
ANCIENT MESOPOTAMIA

The Tigris-Euphrates basin today

1

ANCIENT MESOPOTAMIA: A BIRTHPLACE FOR SCIENCE

In the ancient Near East, civilization began centuries earlier than elsewhere in the world. One small part of this area, ancient Mesopotamia, is often called the cradle of civilization. People began forming permanent settlements there more than eight thousand years ago.

Mesopotamia, which includes the ancient country of Sumer, covered the region we now know as Iraq. Much of the isolated area occupied by the **Sumerian** people lies in the southern portion of a triangle bounded by two rivers, the Tigris and the Euphrates. The Greek roots of the word **Mesopotamia** mean "between the rivers."

This triangle of land, called a delta, was formed by silt and clay carried downstream by the two rivers. The civilization of ancient Mesopotamia grew up around the delta because spring floods promised a yearly supply of silt and nutrients, making the land a fertile spot for agriculture.

The climate of this ancient land was harsh, just as it is today. Eight months might pass without rainfall. Under the merciless summer sun, temperatures reached 110 to 130 degrees Fahrenheit (43 to 54°C) in the shade.

Even so, people came to stay. We know very little about the exact origin of the ancient Sumerians because many groups came to the area from the surrounding mountains, deserts, and seas. These people began thinking and working together and came to form the world's first cities. With permanent settlements, they paid more attention to the world around them and to their place in it. They erected buildings and planted crops. The setting was ripe for learning and discovery.

From at least 3500 B.C. to about 1800 B.C. the Sumerians shaped the culture and civilization of ancient Mesopotamia. By 1800 B.C. a powerful group of invaders made the ancient city of Babylon the center of their rule. The influence of these people—the **Babylonians**—lasted until about 100 B.C.

The world's oldest civilization was also the birthplace of early science and technology. With their creativity and their powers of observation, the people of ancient Mesopotamia helped build a foundation in science for the centuries that followed.

WRITING

*Come, my son, sit at my feet. I will
talk to you, and you will give me
information! Do you know the scribal
art that you have learned?*

No one knows exactly how, where, or when writing began. Simple marks made for counting go back as far as 30,000 years. We do know that in ancient Mesopotamia nature provided the ideal writing material: an endless supply of clay washed downstream by the Tigris and Euphrates Rivers. Soft clay is easily molded into shapes and marked upon with tools.

Writing was first used in ancient Mesopotamia as a form of bookkeeping and counting. Scholars believe the earliest form of writing used small clay counters formed into different shapes. Each small token, whether a sphere, cone, disk, or pyramid, stood for a different quantity: a bushel of grain, a jar of oil, a pot of beer, a fleece of wool, and so on. The tokens were pressed into damp lumps of clay to make impressions that recorded business transactions or land sales.

There were other forms of early writing too. By 3400 B.C. the

Sumerians were drawing small pictures on soft clay to represent facts or objects. Anything important to their lives—grain, fish, oxen, the sun—had its own symbol, or **pictogram.** At about the same time, the ancient Egyptians were also developing their own writing system based on pictograms.

With pictograms, people drew orchards and mountains, oxen and harvests. Because some pictograms stood for several different words, precise meanings might depend on groups of symbols. The Sumerian word *apin,* for example, was a pictogram of a plow. It could have three meanings: "plow," "farmer," or "to cultivate." If the *apin* pictogram appeared with the pictogram *gis* for wood, the combination meant an object made of wood—the plow. If the plow appeared with the pictogram for man, the combination meant "farmer."

FROM PICTOGRAMS TO SYMBOLS AND SOUNDS

Because most pictograms represented simple objects such as a plow, the sun, or a mountain, they couldn't communicate all the details of daily life in ancient Mesopotamia. There was no easy way to combine pictograms to tell about events. Pictograms couldn't tell how quickly the sun moved across the sky, how much water made crops prosper, or why disease might be a sign from the gods. How could a simple picture describe the name of a person or a place? How could it describe time? It certainly couldn't convey complicated thoughts or feelings.

By about 3100 B.C. the Sumerians became the first people to begin adapting picture writing into symbols that stood for syllables and groups of sounds. About a century later, the ancient Egyptians began to rework their early pictograms into more complex **hiero-glyphs,** intricate symbols that they carved in stone or wrote on papyrus, a paperlike material.

As the Sumerian symbols changed through the centuries, they began to look less like small pictures and more like groups of small wedges and lines. The symbol for fish looked very different in 600 B.C. than it did in 3100 B.C.:

about 3100 B.C.	Sumerian about 2500 B.C.	Babylonian		Meaning
		about 1800 B.C.	about 600 B.C.	
				Fish

Development of symbols in ancient Mesopotamia. The three middle boxes contain cuneiform script.

The new symbols were called **cuneiform** script. The wedges and lines formed a kind of shorthand with about five hundred symbols for different sound combinations.

WRITING TOOLS

When writing changed from pictograms to complex symbols, people set aside their pointed drawing sticks. To form the intricate cuneiform signs quickly and in a uniform way, they needed better tools.

Scribes, who spent years learning cuneiform, began using a piece of reed, bone, or wood with a flat, narrow tip. Holding it slightly to the side and pressing hardest at the end, they made wedges or short lines that ended with an indented triangle. For smaller triangles, they pressed with one corner of the blunt tip, and to make dots they poked the opposite, rounded end directly into the clay.

Early scribes wrote in columns, moving from top to bottom and from right to left across their damp tablets. Perhaps to avoid smudging and blurring, they eventually rotated their work a quarter turn to the left, writing across the tablet from left to right. Now the symbols were turned on their sides too, and they looked even less like the objects they once represented.

As the Sumerians refined their symbols, they also became experts at handling clay. They learned how much water to mix with the clay to make it retain sharp impressions of the reed and how much the clay would shrink while drying. They learned to write quickly before their tablets hardened and to keep unfinished writing covered and shielded from the hot sun.

Scribes also made clay envelopes for private messages. As the outer clay layer dried, it shrank to form a tight seal around the tablet inside, something like the seal around a modern medicine bottle. An unbroken clay envelope indicated to the sender and to the receiver that the message had not been read by anyone else.

TABLETS—IN EVERY SHAPE AND SIZE

Tablets recorded information on every topic imaginable, just as books and computer disks do today. There were tablets of astronomical observations, medical instructions, and mathematical formulas. Scribes made long lists of plants, animals, land surveys, and business accounts.

A tablet's purpose—whether it was to convey scientific observations or personal sentiments—often determined its shape and size. Some tablets were round or oval like flattened buns. Others

were square or oblong, or very thin and as small as postage stamps. Larger tablets—some measuring nearly a yard on one side—were sometimes shaped like cushions, with rims of varying thicknesses.

Large tablets were heavy and cumbersome and probably were not carried from place to place. Some served as reference tablets, similar to the large reference books in modern libraries. Because most tablets were small and portable, a simple writing task often required more than one tablet.

A KEY TO THE PAST

While thousands of tablets held mathematical tables, observations of the night sky, or legal documents, they had other purposes too. Some were like postcards, notepads, and letters. They give clues about everyday life in ancient Mesopotamia:

> This is a really fine way of behaving! The orchardists keep breaking into the date storehouse and taking dates, and you yourselves cover it up and do not report it to me . . . bring these men to me—after they have paid for the dates.

Others tell of business difficulties:

> I keep hearing reports that you have sent merchandise to InaSin and Inarawe. Both these men are dead! Although I

Above: *scribes*
Below: *a clay stamp for impressing inscriptions on bricks*

17

searched for evidence for the arrival of any silver, there isn't any. One of you should come here from where you are, or else the silver belonging to your father will be lost.

Until almost A.D. 100 people used cuneiform to preserve every sort of knowledge and experience. They recorded experiments with agriculture, mathematics, and medicine. Scribes faithfully recorded the details of earthquakes, comets, and floods.

For thousands of years afterward, the tablets of Mesopotamia faced scorching heat, burrowing soil organisms, and handling by curious explorers. They survived to tell the story of a great civilization, and they reveal the beginning of science in a small part of the ancient world.

A clay tablet
in an envelope

MEDICINE

Sift and knead together—all in one—
turtle shell, the sprouting naga-plant,
salt [and] mustard; wash [the sick part]
with quality beer [and] hot water; scrub
[the sick part] with all of it [the kneaded
mixture]: after scrubbing, rub with vegetable
oil [and] cover with pulverized fir.

About forty–five hundred years ago, in the ancient city of Nippur, a physician wrote this prescription for an unknown disease. In this and fourteen other carefully written prescriptions, the physician listed materials from nature and stressed cleanliness in caring for patients. He didn't mention that magic might also be a treatment for illness.

DISEASE AND THE GODS

In the ancient Near East, people believed that sickness was caused by demons or was a sign of the gods' displeasure. Sometimes ordinary people were blamed for bringing bad luck to their neighbors by giving them "the evil eye." Most medical treatments were based on trial and error or on folk remedies passed from generation to generation. Many treatments relied on superstition and a belief in magic.

According to the Babylonians, fever came from a demon who entered, then devoured, the body. Although drinking a medicine or spreading an ointment made of ground herbs might make a patient more comfortable, reduce a fever, or slow an infection, the only real cure was to somehow please or pacify the disturbed god.

Because people associated disease with evil, there were two kinds of physicians. The **asu**—the "water-knower"—treated the body and supplied medicines. The **ashipu**—the "conjurer"—was an expert in magic and dealt with the demons and the gods. He knew which gods needed appeasing and offered prayers, sacrifices, chants, and magic rituals as part of a patient's treatment. Despite the division of duties, the ashipu and asu sometimes worked together, combining medicines and chants:

> Let the evil demon leave; let the demons strike at each other. May the good spirit enter the body.

If chants and prescriptions weren't enough to help a patient, the services of a surgeon might be necessary. Surgeons may have held a position separate from that of the typical asu or ashipu.

MESSAGES AND PREDICTIONS

To understand the will of the gods, the Babylonians searched for divine meaning in everyday events. The birth of deformed animals, dreams, shooting stars, or even flights of birds were taken as signs from the gods and interpreted accordingly. Sometimes physicians poured oil into water and used its spreading swirls and odd floating shapes to predict the future, just as some people try to read tea leaves today. By observing signs around them, the Babylonians hoped to gather enough information to change the course of events.

Physicians who tried to drive away the symptoms caused by an angry god learned to look for signs everywhere. To help other physicians, they recorded many of these signs on tablets. Some list signs that the healer might observe on the way to the sick person's home:

If [the physician] sees either a black dog or a black pig, that sick man will die.

If [the physician] sees a white pig, that sick man will live.

If a snake falls on the sick man's bed, that sick man will get well.

If a sick person eventually got well but another person in the family caught the disease, people believed that the demon of the disease had passed from one person to the other. Hoping to give the family some peace, physicians often tried to pass the demon on to animals. They might place a lamb or young goat near the patient and chant the appropriate rites. Later, they killed the animal and cut it open.

If the animal had a diseased liver or lung, or showed any other symptom that might be interpreted as the patient's disease, the physician pronounced the ritual a success. The Babylonians believed the demon and the disease had left the patient.

Perhaps the good news actually helped some patients. Today we know that a positive attitude is an important part of many cures.

LEARNING ABOUT
THE BODY

As physicians looked for signs from the gods in the intestines and organs of animals, they learned the placement of organs, muscle, and other tissue. No doubt the Sumerians and Babylonians also made discoveries from butchering or sacrificing their animals. To learn about the human body in particular, they may have studied the victims of accidents or wars.

Physicians recorded their observations about the human body and its functions. They knew the heart was important, and they considered it to be the center of thought and knowledge. In Babylonian times, people also realized the value of blood as the fluid of life. They discovered that when a body was cut open, much blood was to be found in the liver, the largest, most obvious organ.

The Babylonians considered the liver to be the center of emotions and of life itself. It had an interesting shape, and its five distinct parts, or lobes, could suggest numerous divine signs. To read the signs, Babylonians usually used the livers of sheep or goats, and they gave special names to each lobe. All the features of the liver, whether lines, spots, or wrinkles, had meaning. Reading the liver was so important that the Babylonians made clay models of the organ and covered them with cuneiform inscriptions. The models served as reference tools, illustrating the liver's various abnormalities.

THE FIRST DRUGS

Although ancient physicians left hundreds of prescriptions, the lists of ingredients don't always identify the disease being treated or the dosage of drugs. Scientists think that each physician may have guarded this knowledge carefully or that the details were a matter of trial and error with each patient.

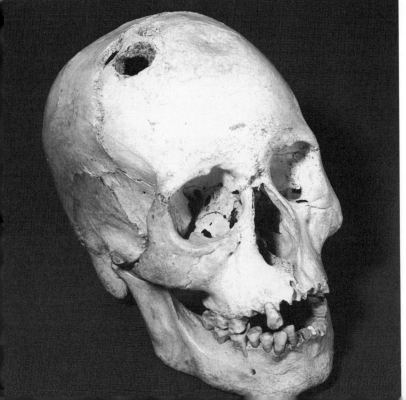

Plant, animal, and mineral matter were important ingredients in early drugs. Common salt was used often in drugs, along with saltpeter. (Saltpeter, whose chemical name is sodium nitrite, is used today as an ingredient in processed meats such as bologna.) Physicians learned to use salt as an antiseptic to clean wounds and saltpeter to help draw torn tissue together.

Milk, snakeskin, and turtle shell found their way into prescriptions, along with herbs such as thyme or plant material from shrubs and trees such as the myrtle, fir, cassia, and willow. Today a bitter chemical found in the bark and leaves of certain willows is an important ingredient in aspirin.

Fruit trees such as the pear, fig, and date were another source of early drugs. Physicians stored seeds, roots, branches, bark, and gum in small batches or ground them into powder to be combined with other ingredients. They often mixed powder with wine or cedar oil to make it spread easily as a salve. Sometimes they added drugs to liquids to be swallowed or dissolved them in beer to hide a disagreeable taste.

EARLY SURGERY

Surgery was not widely practiced, and medical instruments from ancient Mesopotamia often look as if they were adapted from weapons or from women's grooming implements.

Archaeologists have found skulls that show evidence of a surgical practice called **trephination**. If disease caused the brain to

Above: *a clay model of a sheep's liver inscribed with omens and magical formulas* Below: *the hole in this skull was made by trephination.*

swell inside the skull, surgeons sometimes cut out a small piece of skull bone to relieve the pressure. Later, when the swelling had subsided, they replaced the piece. Some skulls showing this kind of surgery are almost seven thousand years old.

THE CODE OF HAMMURABI

Some of the most specific writing about Babylonian surgery comes from the Code of Hammurabi, a group of laws set down by the famous Babylonian king. Hammurabi's laws covered property, business, families, labor, and injuries.

The code required that surgeons be well rewarded if they were successful and punished if they were careless. Rewards or punishments depended on the social class of the patient, however. A surgeon who saved the life of a member of the nobility received ten shekels of silver. For a common citizen, the payment was five shekels; for a slave, two.

A surgeon who caused the death of a person of high rank would have his hand cut off. If the unlucky patient was a slave, the surgeon had to repay the owner the cost of the slave.

SYMPTOMS AND
ANCIENT DISEASE

The Babylonians filled tablet after tablet with lists of symptoms, grouping the symptoms by different organs and body parts. Some

*Hammurabi (standing)
receiving the code of laws
from the god Shamash.
The laws are written
below in cuneiform.*

27

tablets describe symptoms of the eyes, ears, lungs, digestive organs, and muscles. Others give information about childbirth. Tablets describing "the devouring activity of the god," might be referring to epidemics. Sometimes the descriptions of symptoms include the likely fate of the patient:

> If [the sick man] keeps crying out 'My skull! My skull!', [it] is the hand of a god.

> If his brow is white and his tongue is white, his illness will be long, but he will recover.

> If his face is white and overcast with yellow, and his mouth and lips are full of ulcers, and his left eye twitches, he will die.

Although medical treatments clearly depended on signs and superstition, it is often difficult to recognize exactly what diseases afflicted the Sumerians and Babylonians. From carefully studying the tablets, however, cuneiform experts can recognize a few of the more common ailments. They range from serious problems such as mental illness to minor ones such as baldness.

4

MATHEMATICS

Early in their history, the people of ancient Mesopotamia began exploring ways to count, write numbers, and solve numerical problems. By 1800 B.C., the Sumerians had formulated the basic principles of mathematics, an achievement the Greeks did not match until 1,500 years later.

INVENTING
A NUMBER SYSTEM

Even before the Sumerians and Babylonians, ancient people probably used their ten fingers to do simple counting. For that reason, the earliest arithmetic depended on a base ten, or **decimal**, number system like the one we use today. In Mesopotamia, mathematicians went beyond the decimal system and created a more complex system: a **sexagesimal** system. This number system was built around a base of sixty.

In counting and writing, the sexagesimal system of the Sumerians could be confusing, for it actually included features of the decimal system. In the ancient sexagesimal system, the symbol for 1 was Υ , and the symbol for 10 was $\langle$. Simple counting combined the two symbols like this:

$$\Upsilon \ \Upsilon\Upsilon \ \Upsilon\Upsilon\Upsilon \ \overset{\Upsilon\Upsilon}{\Upsilon\Upsilon} \ \overset{\Upsilon\Upsilon}{\Upsilon\Upsilon\Upsilon} \ \overset{\Upsilon\Upsilon\Upsilon}{\Upsilon\Upsilon\Upsilon} \ \overset{\Upsilon\Upsilon\Upsilon}{\Upsilon\Upsilon\Upsilon\Upsilon} \ \overset{\Upsilon\Upsilon\Upsilon\Upsilon}{\Upsilon\Upsilon\Upsilon\Upsilon} \quad \langle \ \langle\Upsilon \ \langle\Upsilon\Upsilon \ \langle\Upsilon\Upsilon\Upsilon$$

1 2 3   4   5   6   7   8   9   10 11 12   13

Counting by tens went like this:

$$\langle \ \langle\langle \ \langle\langle\langle \ \not\langle \ \not\langle\langle$$

10 20 30 40 50

Except for the different symbols, the counting looked very much like it would look in our decimal system. At 60, though, the sexagesimal system took over. The symbol for 60 was Υ , the same as the symbol for 1. So counting from 60 to 80 looked like this:

$$\Upsilon \ \overset{}{\triangleright\!\langle} \ \overset{}{\triangleright\!\langle\langle}$$

60 70 80

In other words, the Sumerians wrote 70 as one group of 60 plus 10; 80 was one group of 60 plus two 10s, and so on. They wrote 120 as two groups of 60, and 130 as two groups of 60 plus one 10:

$$\Upsilon\Upsilon \quad \Upsilon\Upsilon\!\langle$$

120   130

GIVING NUMBERS VALUE

The Sumerians were the first people to give symbols a value depending on their position in a written numeral. Today, for example, when we write the numeral 62, we say that 6 is in the 10's

30

place and that 2 is in the 1's place. Or, put another way, we imagine the number as having six groups of 10 and two 1's. This is the concept of **place value**.

Place value gave scribes an easy way to write large numbers. Because the Sumerians used the position of a numeral to determine its value, their number system had a limited number of symbols. Those symbols could be combined to represent any number, no matter how small or how large.

To see how this idea works, look at the the number 242 in our modern decimal system. The first numeral 2 is in the 100's place, and the last numeral 2 represents units, or 1's. We write both 2s in the same way, using the same symbol. In some ancient cultures, people would have used a different symbol for each of the 2s, simply because they have different place values. Combining all the symbols required to write large numbers could be confusing, because such a system would require many different symbols.

A SYMBOL FOR ZERO

There was one missing element in the sexagesimal number system. For many centuries the Sumerians used the idea of zero, but they had no symbol for it. When they wrote a numeral, if one column or place was empty, they left a blank space. (If we followed this method today, we would write the numeral "504:" as "5 4.") The ancient scribes became concerned that someone recopying their tablets might not notice the empty spaces and might put the figures close together. So they devised a solution.

No one knows exactly when the idea first came about, but mathematical tablets from 300 B.C. or later show that the Babylonians filled the blank spaces with a new symbol that meant "separation." The Babylonians wrote this sign for zero at least two thousand years before the Hindus of India came up with a symbol for nothingness.

PUTTING NUMBERS TO WORK

As ancient Sumerian mathematicians experimented with mathematical ideas, they organized their work on two kinds of tablets. The first type had columns and tables, with row upon row of numbers and calculations. Tablets of this type were very much like the numerical tables in modern textbooks. Some were arranged like multiplication tables, with columns listing multiples of numbers:

$$2 \times 1 = 2$$
$$2 \times 2 = 4$$
$$2 \times 3 = 6$$
$$2 \times 4 = 8$$

and so on. On more complex tablets numbers were squared, or multiplied by themselves:

The square of 1 is 1 ($1 \times 1 = 1$)
The square of 2 is 4 ($2 \times 2 = 4$)
The square of 3 is 9 ($3 \times 3 = 9$)

and so on, until the numbers grew larger:

The square of 8 is 64 ($8 \times 8 = 64$),

or, as the Sumerians would write in their sexagesimal system, $60 + 4$.

Tables that were even more complex listed numbers that mathematicians could insert into mathematical formulas to solve problems.

The second type of tablet used words to describe mathematical problems and sometimes their solutions. Ancient mathematicians wrote problems similar to those in modern textbooks:

Geometry problems. Squares are
divided into various shapes,
and their areas are calculated.

A rectangle. I have multiplied the length by the breadth and have thus obtained the area. I added the length and the breadth and the sum is equal to the area. I added the length, the breadth, and the area, and the total sum of all three is nine. What are the dimensions?

THE MATHEMATICS OF
EVERYDAY LIFE

The mathematicians of ancient Mesopotamia put their knowledge to work in a variety of ways.

The Sumerians and Babylonians were the first people to use their number system as a basis for weights and measures. Mathematics became important in business transactions, for weighing everything from grain to precious metals. We credit the mathematical geniuses of ancient Mesopotamia with dividing the smallest numerical unit into sub-units—the first fractions, which allowed for more precise counting, weighing, and measuring in the course of trading and selling.

Weights were determined by a typical load that could be carried by a person or an animal. This load, called a talent, was divided into 60 minas, and each mina into 60 shekels. A mina weighed about 18 ounces (0.5 kg), and one talent weighed about 67 pounds (30 kg). Sometimes a measurement called a grain was used, a term that reflects the early use of corn to measure both weight and value. Other small weights were expressed as fractions of a shekel.

Measurements of length were based on the **cubit**, which was about 20 inches (0.5 m). The Babylonian mile was more than 6.2 times the length of our modern mile, or more than 10 km. This distance on land was set to equal the Babylonian **double hour**, a length of time about twice as long as our modern hour. Land area was measured by a unit called the field, which is equivalent to

A set of weights (the numbers
are for identification)

about 0.9 acre (0.4 ha). Sometimes areas of land were measured by the quantity of grain needed to sow them.

People learned to use mathematical formulas to calculate the volume of their canals and to plot how much water could be delivered to their parched fields. They learned to measure the area of fields and to divide them into equal portions or fractions of the whole. When floods inundated the land, fields had to be remeasured and re-marked.

The Sumerians and Babylonians devised complex formulas for calculating wages based on work days and fractions of work days. They worked out inheritance problems, deciding how shares of property should be divided among family members, and they computed interest as it accumulated over months and years. On a mathematical tablet almost four thousand years old, one problem asks how long it would take for a sum of money to double at a simple interest rate of 20 percent. (The answer is a little less than four years.)

Complex uses of mathematics were based on early studies of the sky. For a time, some people thought the year had 360 days, a number that can be divided evenly by 60, the base of the sexagesimal number system. As a way to measure time and predict seasons, the Babylonians experimented with mathematical formulas that would predict the movement of the sun, planets, and moon.

Not all formulas and calculations had practical uses. Sometimes mathematicians just experimented, calculating the approximate areas of triangles and circles, or the volumes of cylinders, cones, and pyramids.

One ancient tablet is inscribed with a square and diagonal lines that divide it into four right triangles. Cuneiform symbols show calculations comparing the lengths of the triangle's sides to its hypotenuse, the side opposite the right angle. This tablet is an important discovery. It shows that the Babylonians, not the

Greeks, were the first to use the formula we now call the Pythagorean Theorem. The Babylonians had actually put the formula to use more than a thousand years before the Greek philosopher Pythagoras, for whom it was named.

A KEY TO
THE UNIVERSE

For centuries the people of Mesopotamia juggled between decimal and sexagesimal computation, refusing to be tied to one number system. Although much weighing and measuring was based on the sexagesimal system, some tasks seemed better suited to a decimal system. Sometimes values of measurements or methods of measuring varied from town to town or from one historical period to another.

The mathematical skills of the Sumerians and Babylonians laid a foundation for counting, calculating, weighing, and measuring that influenced other cultures centuries later. With their workable number system, the people of the ancient Near East had a way to measure their observations and record their discoveries. They also had a foundation for studying events in the largest laboratory of all: the sky.

5

EXPLORING THE SKIES

From the earliest times, the people of ancient Mesopotamia had a good reason for watching the sky. They discovered they could measure time by the movement of the stars, planets, and moon. Marking time was important for religious festivals and for planting and harvesting crops. It was also a way to predict the yearly floods of the Tigris and Euphrates Rivers. Flooding meant more than success or failure for crops; it could threaten life as well.

The Sumerians believed that the earth was a flat disk that stood still while gods moved the sun, moon, planets, and stars through the sky, which they imagined was a large dome. Between the earth and sky was the **lil**, or atmosphere, which constantly moved and swirled.

For many centuries, the Babylonians kept detailed records of the movements of planets and stars. In about 400 B.C. they began using mathematics to help predict how the movements changed from month to month or repeated from year to year.

People also watched the heavens for unusual events. From the earliest times they recorded comets as bright lights with glowing tails that traveled across the sky. They noted eclipses, when the moon moved across the face of the sun. They recorded shooting stars and the bright streaks of meteor showers.

Always on the lookout for signs from the gods, the Babylonians believed the sky held important clues to the future. At the beginning of a new year, they made predictions based on the state of the sky:

If the sky is dark, the year will be bad.

If the face of the sky is bright when the new moon appears and [it is greeted] with joy, the year will be good.

If the north wind blows across the face of the sky before the new moon, the corn will grow abundantly.

CREATING A CALENDAR

The Sumerians were patient skywatchers, and their efforts had practical results. They designed a calendar based on the phases of the moon, and the king would announce the beginning of each new month. Each month began just after sunset on the evening when the first thin crescent of moon appeared. Each new Sumerian day began at sunset as well.

Keeping track of time with this calendar could be difficult. At the beginning of some months, bad weather or a cloudy horizon made it hard to see the moon's first thin crescent. If this happened, the king's announcement was postponed for a day or two until astronomers could determine exactly when the first crescent had appeared.

Based on the phases of the moon, the Sumerians had 12 months of about 29½ days each. Their year was 354 days long, or 12 × 29½. Today we know that one year of changing seasons does not depend on when the moon appears. Instead, a year of seasons is related to the earth's movement around the sun. The earth's trip around the sun takes about 365 days, or about eleven more days than the Sumerian year.

By using their year based on the moon's phases, the Sumerians got more and more out of step with the changing seasons. To predict the arrival of seasons, they had to adapt their calendar to keep up with the sun.

The solution was to add an extra month once every three years or so. Up to about 480 B.C. these additions don't seem to have a regular pattern. But by about 400 B.C. the Babylonians had devised a mathematical formula that fit what was happening in the sky. Their formula called for adding seven extra months at equal intervals every nineteen years.

Besides inventing a calendar based on months, the Sumerians were the first people to subdivide the day into parts. A Sumerian day had twelve **double hours**, each broken into thirty parts. Eventually these divisions led to our version of hours and minutes. Dividing an hour into sixty minutes, and the minute into sixty seconds, is a modern use of the sexagesimal number system.

Dividing the day into 360 parts led to another important idea. The circle came to have 360 parts, which we now call degrees.

WATCHING THE NIGHT SKY

As the Babylonians watched the sky they made day-by-day diaries. Some of these observations were used for timekeeping, others for trying to predict the future.

Night after night, month after month, early observers tracked the position of the moon. They recorded how it grew from a thin crescent to a full disk and how it moved among the stars. They noted when bright stars appeared on the horizon and when they disappeared from sight. And they recorded a number of imaginary objects and animals outlined by stars. Among these figures, which

A table recording the motions of Jupiter

we call constellations, are Draco the Dragon, Sirius the Dog Star, and Leo the Lion.

The planets Mercury, Venus, Mars, Jupiter, and Saturn intrigued the Babylonians. They were bright points of light that seemed to travel among the fixed patterns of the dimmer stars. The ancient people playfully compared the wandering planets with wild sheep and the stars with tame sheep.

Just as the earth was divided into kingdoms, the Babylonians considered the sky as having three great zones. Each was named after an important god. The central zone swept diagonally across the sky and was called the "way of Anu." To the north of it was the "way of Enlil"; to the south was the "way of Ea." Within these zones the Babylonians recorded and named visible stars and constellations.

The early observers realized that the sun, moon, and planets all travel through the sky along roughly the same path. By about 450 B.C. they had made this path part of an imaginary, diagonal strip across the sky called the zodiac. They divided the zodiac into twelve segments and named each one after a nearby constellation.

With a few exceptions, our modern Latin names for the zodiac signs come from Greek translations of the old Babylonian names. They include Aries (the Hired Man), Taurus (the Bull of Heaven), Gemini (the Great Twins), Cancer (the Crab), Leo (the Lion), Virgo (the Barley Stalk), Libra (the Balance), Scorpio (the Scorpion), Sagittarius (the god Pablisag), Capricorn (the Goatfish), Aquarius (the Giant), and Pisces (the Tails).

As the sun traveled through the sky during the course of a year, it remained for one month in each of the twelve segments of the zodiac. The Babylonians noted that the sun spent three months in the "path of Enlil" in the summer, and another three months in the "path of Anu." It spent three months in the "path of Ea" in the winter, and then three more months in the "path of Anu."

As a result of their careful observations, the Babylonians were able to calculate when planets traveled into each sign of the zodiac. For astrologers, people who used the sky to predict the future, the zodiac provided endless possibilities for speculation.

MEASURING DISTANCE AND TIME

The Babylonians used bright stars as reference points to describe the positions of other stars. They also took measurements based on time, with the help of a device called the **clepsydra.** The clepsydra was a kind of water clock that measured time by the weight of dripping water. To determine the distance between two stars, astronomers first imagined a line stretching from the point in the sky directly above them down to the horizon. This perpendicular line, called a meridian, would serve as a reference point.

As the night wore on, constellations moved across the sky. First one star, then others, would move across the meridian. Meanwhile, water slowly dripped through the clepsydra. The amount of water dripping from the time one star crossed the meridian to the time another crossed was used as a measure of distance between them. With this method, the entry on a tablet might read something like this: "Two and a half minas [the weight of the water] from Gamlu to the constellation of Gemini."

Sometimes the Babylonians used a type of **sundial** to help track the sun's movement. The sundial probably had a flat, horizontal base with a pointed stick stuck into it. As the sun moved across the sky, the stick cast a moving shadow along curved lines on the base. Different curved lines were drawn to represent the shadow of the sun on the longest and shortest days of the year.

Using observations like these, the Babylonians tried to calculate the length of the shadow from a vertical bar at different times of the year and day. They also experimented with formulas for calculating the times of the rising and setting of the moon.

WATCHING AN
AGE-OLD COMET

Skywatchers also faithfully tracked the movements of comets, sometimes describing which way the tails pointed. The story of one such comet has been especially fascinating for modern astronomers. It's the comet we know today as Halley's Comet, named after the British astronomer Edmund Halley.

Halley's Comet becomes visible from earth every seventy-six years. By using ancient records, historians and astronomers have traced its visits as far back as 12 B.C. Until recently, the records stopped there. By making adjustments for different calendar systems, astronomers predicted that earlier appearances should have come in 164 B.C. and 87 B.C. Then, they took a closer look at a collection of ancient Babylonian tablets stored in London's British Museum.

On tablets and fragments of tablets were descriptions of comets that had appeared in 164 B.C. and 87 B.C. It looked as though modern astronomers had found the oldest records of Halley's Comet!

To test their theory, the astronomers rechecked daily diaries kept by the Babylonians. They studied the dates of eclipses, the positions of planets, and the movement of the moon. Then they checked the times and positions with modern calculations. Finally they were certain that the Babylonians had indeed recorded the appearances of Halley's Comet.

6

SURVEYING NATURE

For the people of ancient Mesopotamia the earth must have held as much fascination as the skies. As far back as 3000 B.C. the Sumerians began keeping lists of plants, wild and domesticated animals, rocks, and minerals. Just as modern bird watchers record each species they encounter, the Sumerians patiently and persistently recorded life around them. For these ancient people, making lists was a way to organize the world and make it seem orderly and predictable. They learned what plants could be used for drugs, what rocks made the best flagstones, what kinds of fish were best for eating.

Sometimes the ancient listmakers grouped living species in strange or surprising ways, with definitions of animals, plants, and minerals that were unclear. In one case, a stone, a piece of hail, and a date pit all belong to the same list!

For modern scientists, these ancient lists of plants and animals are more than curiosities. They give important clues to how people lived, how they ate, and how living populations changed through the centuries.

Vines and flowers

THE WORLD OF PLANTS

Scribes sometimes listed plants by their appearance, describing their leaves and flowers, then including a specific name. Perhaps these tablets served as ancient reference books. Other times scribes listed plants by their uses. Those used in making ointments or salves might be grouped together and identified by a symbol meaning "scent." Other lists group plant names as if they were entries in a dictionary. Some lists don't seem to have a logical order at all; perhaps each was just a collection of random observations.

Sometimes the ancient people chose plant names to match their idea of familiar body parts, just as we do today. The ancient plant called "hound's tongue" might not be the same hound's tongue we know today, however.

In one lush garden, the Babylonians raised plants, grouping them by their uses or common features. The Garden of Merodach-Baladan, a Babylonian king, was home for both common vegetables and exotic plants.

Garlic, leeks, and onions were in one group, and herbs such as basil and mint in another. Seasonings such as saffron, coriander, and thyme grew together, and in another part of the plot were melons and gourds. Lettuce and endive thrived side by side, while lentils, beets, carrot-like vegetables, and fennel bulbs all had their place.

There were fruit trees, too. Date palms shared space with pomegranates. Small trees such as apricot, plum, peach, and fig were planted together to shield vegetables from the scorching sun.

ANIMALS AND FISH

Just as they grouped plants by type, the Sumerians made lists of animals: fish, snakes, birds, four-legged creatures, and so on. Along with designs painted on pottery, these lists tell us which animals roamed wild in ancient Mesopotamia. One was a small horse with a camel-like head and a short, stiff mane. Another was a humped ox, an animal native to India. Its presence in Mesopotamia shows there was very early contact between the two countries. A long-bearded ram with widely separated and curved horns also makes its appearance. This graceful creature has long since become extinct.

Besides observing wild animals, people also recorded nature as it affected their everyday lives. In ancient Mesopotamia fish was a major source of food, especially if crops failed. Fish were so important that people identified more than a hundred different types. One ancient list from about 2000 B.C. names eighteen edible varieties sold in the marketplace at Larsa, a town near the Persian Gulf. These fish came from lagoons near the shore as well as from artificial canals.

One unusual cuneiform tablet describes a "house built for fish," perhaps the huge net of a fisherman. The writer describes a large, safe place that is well stocked with food. He tries to lure a number of fish inside to enjoy it: "My Fish, may all kinds of fish enter with you."

In all, the ancient writer names sixteen different fish, including carp, sturgeon, catfish, and eels. All are urged to come quickly to their new home, because danger lurks nearby from fish-eating birds and sharks.

ROCKS AND MINERALS

Ancient people also turned their attention to rocks and the individual minerals that form them. These they grouped by appearance as well as by uses. Some stones intrigued the Sumerians because of their great beauty. Others were important because they could be shaped into tools, split for paving stones, or stacked as building blocks.

Instead of carefully describing the features of different stones, one ancient story explains their names and uses:

Ninurta, a great god, was taken by surprise as a group of his enemies threatened him. All around, the stones of the earth took sides: some for Ninurta, some against him. When Ninurta had won the battle, he turned to the stones, giving them names and rewarding or punishing them for their actions.

To the loyal stones, he gave beautiful names and fine textures. From that time on, these would be the stones used for making statues and building altars. They would be the ornaments of worship or the precious stones of jewelry. Marble, alabaster, lapis lazuli, crystalline quartz, jasper, carnelian, and many others were among the prized stones.

The hostile, disloyal stones were not so lucky. They became the common stones—the rough, dull, unnoticed stones used to pave streets and frame entryways. Or, worst of all, they became the worthless stones that remained as pebbles in the road.

7

TECHNOLOGY FOR EVERYDAY LIFE

Ancient Mesopotamia was a land of technology. Its people invented the wheel before 4000 B.C., and they made pottery, bricks, and metal objects, along with complicated plows, chariots, and musical instruments. The people of ancient Mesopotamia established a thriving wool industry as early as 4000 B.C., complete with bleaching, spinning, dyeing, and weaving. They invented an alcoholic drink made of dates, and from barley they learned to brew beer, the drink that "makes the liver happy and fills the heart with joy." (Actually, alcohol turns out to be *bad* for the liver.) The world's oldest recipe, written on a tablet in about 1750 B.C., is for beer.

By 3000 B.C. the Sumerians had made the first soap from vegetable oils. To make other substances used for medicine, magic rituals, or cosmetics, early chemists used crucibles, filtering vessels, and drip bottles. They also made incense and perfume, often guided by women who developed the recipes.

Leather tanning was a technology guided by prescribed rituals. Animal skins were soaked in liquids and rubbed with fats and oils to make them soft and flexible. The finished leather was used for harnesses and sandals, or to make pouches for drinking water, milk, and butter. Inflated skins served as "floats" to help swimmers cross rivers.

AGRICULTURE IN MESOPOTAMIA

Raising food was the most important activity of all. The world's earliest known farming communities were in the upper valley of the Euphrates River and in the foothills surrounding Mesopotamia. By 6000 B.C. people were growing crops such as wheat and barley, and they had cultivated their land with the first plows. They also raised the basic herd animals: sheep, goats, cattle, and pigs.

Centuries later, beekeepers had learned to collect honey from wild bees and to separate it from the beeswax:

> I introduced the flies which collect honey, which in the time of my predecessors nobody knew nor introduced, and located them in the garden of the town Gabbarini that they might collect honey and wax; I even understood how to separate the honey from the wax by boiling; my gardeners also knew this.

From the earliest days, one of the most widespread agricultural practices in Mesopotamia was shade tree gardening. Farmers planted broad shade trees to protect their garden plants from the sun and wind. And while they didn't use manure to fertilize their fields, farmers sometimes added rubble from old bricks to improve the soil. People in the Near East still follow this practice today.

One Sumerian farmer left a kind of handbook for his son, describing yearly agricultural activities and offering suggestions for the younger man. On the cuneiform tablet, the farmer tells his son that fields must be cleared of weeds, then fenced. The son should also have an extra ox for the plow.

51

Plowing with an ox

Before plowing, the ground must be broken up twice by the pick and once by the hoe; if large clumps of earth remain, they should be broken up with a hammer. The father tells his son to stand over the laborers to make certain they do not shirk their work.

Plowing and sowing seeds were done at the same time. The plow had an attachment to carry seeds from a container through a narrow funnel, down to the furrow. The farmer warns his son that seeds must be placed at an even depth. After the seeds are sown, clumps of hard earth should be broken or cleared again so they will not block the sprouting barley.

Once the seeds sprouted, the young farmer should say a prayer to Ninkilim, the goddess of field mice and vermin, so that rodents would not harm the growing grain. The farmer tells his son to water the grain and to harvest it before its tops bend over from their weight. Finally, the father informs his son that these rules and directions are those of the god Ninurta, a "true farmer" and son of the god Enlil.

IRRIGATION

Mesopotamia became one of the richest granaries in the ancient world. Wheat, barley, dates, and a variety of other fruits and vegetables thrived. Crops were often traded for stone, metals, or other goods from neighboring lands.

But farming the fertile crescent between the two great rivers was not an easy task. At the end of summer's dry season, the rivers trickled slowly through a desolate land of sun-baked mud. Winter rainstorms brought more water to the rivers, but not nearly a full load. By spring, melting snow from the nearby mountains fed the tributaries, and floods threatened the river plain and its crops. This almost uncontrollable surge of water usually came between April and June—too late for watering the bulk of the crops, which were ready for harvest in April.

The solution was irrigation, routing water to dry land. The Sumerians became skilled engineers, digging ditches and building a complex system of canals, reservoirs, and dikes. Huge canals connected the river tributaries, and smaller canals branched off. Smaller irrigation ditches tapped water from the canals, making the land a maze of artificial waterways. To irrigate their smaller gardens, farmers used simple water-lift devices, a method still used in Iraq today. The entire system was so well-designed that directing water wherever it was needed was easy.

There was another advantage too. By quickly distributing excess water, the web of canals and irrigation ditches provided built-in protection from floods.

But skilled technology couldn't completely control the power of running water. Harnessing the rivers meant fighting a constant battle with nature. Canals and ditches quickly filled with silt and clay, which had to be scooped out and piled on nearby banks. And even then the problem wasn't solved. Piles of silt along the canal banks became so high that new canals had to be dug alongside the old ones. Today, airplane passengers can see an amazing network formed by the ancient channels. Some have as many as three sets of canals, lined side by side.

Even in ancient times, technology had its negative side. River water was high in salt, and as it evaporated the salt stayed behind as a white crust in the fields. In areas of heavy agriculture, salt built up faster than rainwater could carry it away. Farmers began growing more barley, which tolerates salt better than wheat. When barley could no longer grow, farmers moved to new ground, and the destructive process began again.

By 2000 B.C. the Sumerians had begun experimenting with ways to fight the salt problem or at least slow its damage. At the same time, they were learning other ways to make agriculture more productive. An agricultural manual from 2100 B.C. describes simple methods of draining land and of letting fields rest for a season or more between plantings.

CLAY: RESOURCE
AND TOOL

Although clay was a problem for irrigation, it was also the most valuable resource in ancient Mesopotamia. Clay was the basic material for a writing system that left hundreds of thousands of tablets. Pots and jugs were made of clay; so were small statues and figurines. Clay was also the building material for homes and public structures. Because metal was not abundant, the earliest sickles for cutting barley were often made of baked clay.

It was easy to form the first small pinch pot from soft clay, just by pushing and pressing it into a small bowl shape. But making strong, durable pottery demanded special skill.

Clay for making pottery or tablets had to be clean. If it wasn't, the Sumerians washed it by dropping handfuls into water and stirring. As small pieces of wood, leaves, and straw floated to the top, potters skimmed them off. They also removed the coarser sand and pebbles that quickly sank. After a while, a clean layer of clay settled to the bottom of the container and the water could be easily poured off.

Pots and jars made with fine, clean clay were relatively sturdy. But to hold liquids and be durable for long periods, they had to be fired. Firing at high temperatures causes individual clay particles to fuse together. These particles are composed mostly of silica, the same mineral used to make glass. Fired pottery has a hard, glasslike appearance.

Through the centuries, the skill of potters grew. Instead of forming pots entirely by hand, they learned to make graceful shapes on the potter's wheel, a tool invented in ancient Mesopotamia. Complex geometric lines and figures decorated pottery called "scarlet ware," which had bright red and black paint over a yellowish background. Potters also experimented to find the best firing temperatures so pottery could be strong as well as beautiful.

BUILDING WITH CLAY

As a building material, clay was abundant and inexpensive. Most of the buildings in ancient Mesopotamia were made of sun-dried bricks stacked and held together by mortar made of mud.

Brickmaking didn't require the fine, clean clay used for pottery. The Sumerians learned they could use coarser clay that contained some sandy particles. To reinforce its strength, they mixed the clay with finely chopped straw, then poured it into plain wooden molds.

The Sumerians were the first people to use brick molds to shape uniform bricks. When the new bricks were nearly dry, brickmakers removed the molds to let the bricks dry in open air. Drying went quickly, especially in the summer. Siwan, the first summer month, was also called "the month of the bricks." Like pottery, bricks were stronger when fired. However, if fuel was scarce, only the bricks of larger, more important buildings got this special treatment.

People, especially the kings, were proud of their architecture. Sometimes fired bricks were stamped or inscribed so that people would remember the current king for his great building projects. If the inscriptions were hard to see, builders added another technique to their skills: they used clay nails. Some of these nails had heads several inches in diameter, large enough to hold an inscription praising the king. Stuck in the soft mortar between layers of bricks, the fired nails became a permanent form of praise for the king who had built or repaired the building.

TOWERS ON THE PLAINS

As people perfected the art of making and baking mudbricks, their buildings grew taller and more impressive. They built large, towerlike brick structures called **ziggurats** for religious purposes. One such tower was built at the ancient city of Nippur as a shrine to the god Enlil.

The Sumerians were the first people to build arches and domes, but they didn't master the art of building straight, narrow towers. Instead, they built story upon story, each slightly smaller than the one below it. A broad stairway stretched to the top of the ziggurat, where the temple was situated.

GLASS: A NEW MATERIAL

Although clay was a versatile material, the Sumerians knew it couldn't meet all their needs. As early as 3000 B.C., the Sumerians had explored the properties of chemicals like lime (which contains calcium) and soda (which contains sodium), as well as the **silicate** minerals—those made up of intricate networks of silicon and oxygen atoms. Sand is made mostly of silicate minerals. At high temperatures, individual particles fuse and become glassy, just like fired clay.

By combining lime, soda, silicates, and other minerals, craftspeople made colorful glazes for pottery. Gemstones were scarce, so they made substitutes by painting quartz pebbles with blue and green mineral colors that changed to a permanent glaze after firing. They also learned to make a new material: glass. Although glass wasn't nearly as common as pottery in ancient Mesopotamia, the Sumerians experimented with chemical formulas to make different colors.

Like certain medical prescriptions or technologies that depended on special formulas, the details of glassmaking may have

The ziggurat of Ur, restored

been kept secret. The earliest known recipe for glass comes from the Babylonians and is written in odd signs that some archaeologists interpret as secret symbols. It would not be unusual for tablets to contain cryptic or misleading instructions or scattered codewords known only to craftspeople.

USING METAL

Although ancient Mesopotamia lacked rocks containing copper or other metals, the Sumerians became expert metal workers. Arabia, Persia, or the highlands of Syria and Turkey are likely sources for the metal that was imported to the ancient Near East in return for grain, wool, or other goods.

The Sumerians discovered that metal could be hammered and stretched into different shapes. And, just as with pottery and glass, they learned that metal could be changed and strengthened at high temperatures. Metalsmiths probably used bellows to blow air onto hot coals, and it's likely they added charcoal to help fires reach the high temperatures necessary for working metal.

By 3000 B.C., ancient metalsmiths worked with copper, silver, gold, and some bronze, a mixture, or **alloy**, made by adding tin to copper. By about 2500 B.C. the Sumerians had discovered how important bronze could be. The new alloy was harder than pure copper, yet it could be adapted to many uses, from weapons to tools to jewelry.

It wasn't until about 1000 B.C. that metalsmiths began using iron, which at first they retrieved from meteorites. Although iron was a new material to the ancients, its use spread slowly, for it could not be adapted to as many uses as bronze.

Metalsmiths had to provide tools for farming, weapons, objects for the temple, and ornaments for people. They hammered copper into spears, daggers, and shields. They made knives, drill bits, pins, chisels, and axe blades.

The same craftspeople also made cups, vases, highly decorated combs, earrings, and large, ornate headdresses. Sometimes they hammered gold, turning it into elegant helmets and shaping locks of hair in the soft metal. By using a pointed tool and a technique called chasing, they pressed thin, intricate lines in the metal—in the same way a pencil drawn across aluminum foil creates a thin, raised ridge. In this way, metalsmiths "drew" human hairs as decoration on golden helmets.

For some of these objects, the Sumerians used a technique called casting. By pouring molten metal into molds, they made everyday tools and utensils, as well as small, elegant statues and figurines. The complex molding of some of these works of art shows that Sumerian metalsmiths were highly skilled at their craft.

GEOGRAPHY AND MAP MAKING

The people of ancient Mesopotamia were curious about how their land fit into the world and the universe. More than forty-five hundred years ago the Sumerians drew maps on clay tablets to show the courses of rivers and the locations of seas. Other maps, which cover very small areas of ground, were probably meant to outline the exact boundaries of estates or fields.

The Sumerians left a map of the ancient city of Nippur that is amazingly easy to decipher. Its lines are so accurate that modern archaeologists used it to plan their excavations.

Some maps, like the Babylonian version of the world, require more imagination to read. Mesopotamia and its neighbors are drawn as a circular plain surrounded by water. At the center of the plain is the city of Babylon, and scattered around it are small circles that represent other cities. Triangles that stretch outside the circle of Mesopotamia refer to nearby countries.

A Babylonian map of the world
from the seventh century B.C.
Babylon is at the center.

8

THE LEGACY OF ANCIENT MESOPOTAMIA

The heritage of ancient Mesopotamia is everywhere. It lives on in the way we communicate, the way we study science, and in our everyday lives.

By transforming simple pictograms into more complex symbols based on syllables and sound, the Sumerians took the first steps toward representing spoken language with written symbols. They made writing a tool for knowledge that could be passed from generation to generation.

The Sumerians and Babylonians shaped abstract ideas into mathematical reality, setting down the basic principles of mathematics centuries before other cultures. They invented a complex sexagesimal number system whose best features serve us today when we divide the circle into 360 degrees, each degree into 60 minutes, and each minute into 60 seconds. The sexagesimal system also lives on in the division of our day into hours, minutes, and seconds.

From the Sumerians and Babylonians we inherited fractions, along with the idea of weights and measures based on a number system. Built around the sexagesimal system, this system of weights and measures outdid all similar systems among ancient people—and it didn't face major alteration until modern times. From the Babylonians come the first complex formulas for solving mathematical problems. Other major achievements, the idea of place values and a written symbol for zero, are keys to making any complex number system work.

In astronomy, precise record keeping is the greatest single contribution from Mesopotamia. Without tablets and day-to-day accounts of the ancient skies, today's astronomers would be missing several thousand years of data. By studying cuneiform tablets, modern scientists have expanded their knowledge of astronomy, tracing ancient eclipses, appearances of comets, and movements of planets. Each time we observe familiar constellations, we can recall that the Babylonians were the first to name these groupings of stars.

The ancient Mesopotamians, in observing nature, compiled the first lists and simple classifications of plants and animals. With the invention of the plow and irrigation, large-scale agriculture became possible.

The people of Mesopotamia invented the wheel and became the first chemists, developing formulas for making glass and casting metal. The world's oldest pottery comes from ancient Mesopotamia, land of the first potter's wheel. And it was here that people used the first brick molds and first began to build with fired bricks.

The people of ancient Mesopotamia left an inheritance of ideas to shape our knowledge of astronomy, mathematics, medicine, and agriculture. They also left a wealth of information for modern scientists who study the ancient world. Using cuneiform tablets and everyday objects that survived the centuries, scientists have pieced together the daily life of a great culture in a land that was truly the cradle of civilization.

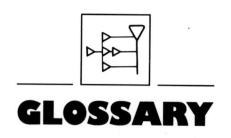

GLOSSARY

Alloy: A material made by combining two or more metals. See **Bronze.**

Ashipu: A healer who dealt with gods and demons and offered prayers, chants, or rituals as a treatment for illness.

Asu: A physician who treated the body and supplied medicines.

Babylonian: The people and culture that flourished in ancient Mesopotamia beginning in about 1800 B.C.

Bronze: A yellowish-brown mixture, or alloy, of copper and tin.

Clepsydra: A clock that uses dripping water to measure time.

Cubit: An ancient measure of length usually based on the length of the forearm from the elbow to the tip of the middle finger. The Babylonian cubit was about 20 inches (0.5 m).

Cuneiform: The system of writing developed in ancient Mesopotamia. It was based on wedge-shaped characters and was most often inscribed on clay tablets.

Decimal: A base-ten number system. The number system we use today for counting and computation is a decimal system.

Double hour: A measure of time approximately twice as long as the modern sixty-minute hour.

Hieroglyphs: Symbols used in the ancient Egyptian form of writing, where figures or objects represent words or sounds.

Lil: The swirling, expanding material that the Sumerians believed was between the earth and the dome of the heavens.

Pictogram: An ancient written symbol in the form of a picture. Pictograms represented the sun, grain, fish, and other common objects.

Place value: The value given to the location of a digit in a numeral. In 34, for example, the location of the digit 3 has a place value of ten. The digit itself indicates three tens.

Sexagesimal: A system of counting and mathematical computation based on the number 60.

Silicate: A mineral whose structure is composed largely of silicon and oxygen atoms; also, rocks composed of these minerals.

Sumerian: The people and culture that built the civilization of ancient Mesopotamia, beginning about 3500 B.C. or earlier.

Sundial: A device that shows the path of the sun or the time of day by a shadow cast on a horizontal base.

Trephination: A surgical practice that called for cutting out a small piece of the skull to relieve pressure caused by swelling of the brain. Once the swelling subsided, the piece of bone was replaced.

Ziggurat: A temple tower built by the ancient Babylonians. Each successive story has a smaller area, giving the tower a pyramid-like appearance.

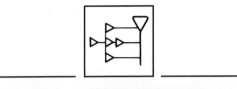

FOR FURTHER READING

Chiera, Edward. *They Wrote on Clay*. Chicago: University of Chicago Press, 1966.

Cottrell, Leonard. *Land of the Two Rivers*. Cleveland: World Publishing, 1962.

Heyerdahl. Thor. *The Tigris Expedition: In Search of Our Beginnings*. New York: Doubleday, 1981.

Kramer, Samuel Noah. *History Begins at Sumer*. Philadelphia: University of Pennsylvania Press, 1981.

Lloyd, Seton. *The Archaeology of Mesopotamia*. London: Thames and Hudson, 1984.

Lloyd, Seton. *Foundations in the Dust: The Story of Mesopotamian Exploration*. London: Thames and Hudson, 1980.

Lloyd, Seton. *The Ruined Cities of Iraq*. Chicago: Ares, 1980.

Oates, Joan. *Babylon*. London: Thames and Hudson, 1979.

Oppenheim, A. Leo. *Letters from Mesopotamia*. Chicago: University of Chicago Press, 1967.

Woolley, C. Leonard. *The Sumerians*. New York: Norton, 1965.

SOURCES OF QUOTATIONS

p. 12: John Oates, *Babylon* (London: Thames and Hudson, 1979).

p. 17, 19: A. Leo Oppenheim, *Letters from Mesopotamia* (Chicago: University of Chicago Press, 1967).

p. 20: Elizabeth Lansing, *The Sumerians* (New York: McGraw-Hill, 1971).

p. 21: Charles Seignobos, *The World of Babylon* (New York: Leon Amiel, 1975).

p. 22, 28: H.W.F. Saggs, *The Greatness That Was Babylon* (London: Sidgwick and Jackson, 1962).

p. 34: Georges Contenau, *Everyday Life in Babylon and Assyria* (London: Edward Arnold, 1959).

p. 39: B.L. van der Waerden, "Mathematics and Astronomy in Mesopotamia," in: C.C. Gillespie (ed.), *Supplement* to the *Dictionary of Scientific Biography*, vol. 15 (New York: Scribner's, 1978).

p. 51: John Oates, *Babylon*.

INDEX

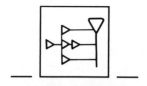

ABOUT
THE AUTHOR

Carol Moss is a freelance science writer living in St. Paul, Minnesota. This is her first book for Franklin Watts.